CRIC EXPLORE 3 (2022 edition)

A Complete Guide To Master Explore 3, Learn How To Use Cricut Design Space, And Create Amazing DIY Projects

By

Natasha Waku

Table of content

INTRODUCTION

Cricut Explore 3 is Cricut's latest, best-selling cutting machine. It is an upgrade from the previous version, Cricut Explore Air 2. You may be wondering where the 'Air' disappear to? Well, 'Air' was initially added to show the machine had Bluetooth (wireless) capabilities, but Cricut figured it's best to remove it since almost every device has Bluetooth connectivity.

The upgrades on this new cutting machine makes it perfect for both beginners and advanced crafters. It enables users to cut larger designs, cut materials such as cardboards, papers, and vinyl. It is also used for cutting thin leathers, foams, magnet sheets, fabrics, even woods (less than 2mm thick).

With this new machine from Cricut, there is really little that can be achieved in the way of DIY crafting.

In this instruction guide, you will learn how to use the new Cricut Explore 3. You will get easy to follow directions, designed to guide you as you start using the machine to create your own designs.

Lets get right to it!!

CHAPTER ONE

What exactly is a Cricut Machine?

A Cricut is a machine known for its cutting ability. A Cricut can cut various paper products, plastic, cardboards, and iron-on transfers into varying styles. Even leather and wood can be cut with certain Cricut machines. A Cricut is a machine that can slice a range of paper products, plastic, and cardboard for your DIY projects. It is this cutting ability that gives the Cricut its efficiency as a crafting machine. Because the Cricut machine can cut a wide range of materials, it allows you to easily make designs and crafts from all these various materials.

It enables anyone to cut and make beautiful crafts out of basically anything. Depending on the type Cricut machine you possess, you might also sketch, imprint, and construct folded patterns to create three-dimensional crafts, birthday cards, and packages.

You can liken it to a printer in some ways. This is because you can generate an image and print it out. Besides, it doesn't produce your layout; instead, it cuts it from whatever material you wish!

What Is the Purpose of a Cricut Machine?

Cricut machines are popular among craftspeople for:

- Iron T-Shirt, Clothes, and Tote Bag Add-Ons
- Coffee cups, drinking glasses, as well as other serving utensils
- Projects for Papercrafting and Scrapbooking
- Wooden signs
- Projects for Important Events like Bridal Shower or Engagement Stickers for Organizers (or just for pleasure!) Vinyl Decals for your house or on your car
- Gifts for Babies.

Types and Features of a Cricut Machine

There are five major Cricut machines available right now:

The Cricut Maker

This is the ideal cutter for all of your crafts requirements; it can swiftly and correctly cut various materials, from sensitive material and papers to mats boards and leather. Oh, and don't worry, it still shreds plastic and iron-on stuff! So it is a one-stop shop for all your crafting needs.

The Cricut Maker 3

Without alienating consumers, the Cricut Maker 3 improves accessibility and convenience. One other modest obstacle to usage has been eliminated with the addition of Cricut Smart Materials; consumers can now strive to create and enhance their craft basics. In addition, the extensive design options will provide lots of choices if you can bear some minor difficulties and restrictions with the Design Space software.

Cricut Joy

Cricut Joy cuts writes, and sketches for you to add joy to daily tasks like organizing your house and adding your personalized feel to practically everything. Get started right away on tasks like stickers, decals, and postcards. Each day, you'll come up with new ways to customize, arrange, and modify your life. That is correct; we're betting you'll take a break from your inspiration walls and get down to business.

Cricut Explore Air 2

This one has some fantastic features. For example, you may choose 3,000 prepared creations or build your own. The pre-designed items include everything, including a supply list and guidelines.

Cricut Access Standard gives you easy accessibility to over 370 typefaces, more than 30,000 photos, and some exclusives. You'll also get a 10% discount on your buys. Isn't that exciting?

The Cricut Explore Air 2 is cloud-based; you are able to construct a craft from any desktop, smartphone, tablet, or cellphone.

Cricut Explore 3

What makes the Cricut Explore 3 unique is its use of current smart materials and its excellent cutting ability of about 12 feet in length. It is equally about two times speedier than the Explore Air 2 cutting smart materials.

Because the Explore 3's material settings are already merged into the program, Cricut was able to eliminate the dials from the machine, resulting in a sleeker and much more polished design. It also received a sensor upgrade, allowing it to cut projects on brown and white paper.

CHAPTER TWO

The Cricut Explore 3

These versatile tools accommodate countless possibilities for making crafts on almost any material. However, just before we go deep into this fantastic cutting machine, let's check out some of its features that set it apart from its previous version.

- It cuts at speed twice (2X) as fast.
- It comes with smart materials; you don't need a mat.
- It can handle materials 13 inches wide and up to 75 feet.
- It has a built mobile device stand to hold your devices.
- It has a design space app that can be installed on your PC and mobile devices for designing the output you want. You can upload

images and designs for the machine to cut out with the design space. You also get access to its ready-made libraries of fonts, images, and designs.

- It can cut, write, score, and foil.

- There is provision for a roll holder (though sold separately) to help keep the Smart Materials organized and aligned for clean, precise cuts.

- It can support two tool heads, making two different tasks concurrently on the same project.

- It allows a smooth connection between your device and the machine via Bluetooth. Cricut Explore 3 also has a cable to connect your PC directly, giving you connection options to pick from.

- White and colored paper can be printed on and cut by Cricut Explore 3. This isn't possible with Cricut Explore Air 2 as only white paper can be printed on and cut.

Unboxing

On opening the sleek box of your device, you find four essential things in it; a white envelope, a pack of useful smart materials, the Cricut Explore 3 itself, and the USB and Power Adapter cable. Well, go back if you missed the headline on the carton, 'You were born creative.' Just kidding!

Now within the white envelope holds necessary documents, which will make using your Cricut Explore 3 device a smooth one.

- A green info card. This essentially is a get started card, beautifully written on it - in three different languages, take a pick - that directs you to www.cricut.com/setup. This gives you a summary of how to get your device up and running without any hitches. Wonderful, right?

- A warranty and safety information card. Did you know that your Cricut Explore 3 has a warranty of one year? Now you know.

- A smart vinyl material. Very thoughtful of them. You have a Cricut Smart Vinyl material to carry a test cut as a sample. So get creative and follow the guidelines on creating art!

Inside the Ziploc bag, you will find a package of bonus smart materials. These are Smart Paper Sticker Card Stock, Smart Iron-On (color may differ), Smart Vinyl, and Transfer Tape to go with it.

Lastly, you have your USB cable and your Power Cable. Notice that your Power cable is more portable than what usually is in Explore Air 2. These cables go into the back of your machine with the other end of the USB cable into your device.

New Features

It has been a long time we said goodbye to glue and getting our hands dirty while trying to be creative. But life keeps getting better with all these smart machines being produced daily, no complaints here. Cricut ensured they came back bigger and better, as compared to previous models, with the following qualities:

If time was ever an issue for you before, then the Cricut Explore 3 is for you. The inbuilt motors are created to work twice as fast as before using Smart materials and with such incredible precision.

Also, you do not need a mat. While a mat takes in the regular material to be cut while still regulating the amount of material that can be cut, the Cricut Explore 3 does not need this mat yet can take in as much as 12ft of your Smart Vinyl.

The top has a little inlet for holding your iPad or phone, as you desire, while you cut. Looking at the right side of the machine, you would notice that the manual dial and port are no longer there. Instead, it has been neatly replaced with some fine set of buttons; the Power button, the Load/Unload button, the Go button, and the Pause button.

Since the machine works better with Smart materials, it does not need the dial anymore. Instead, it has a sensor that detects the size of the material to be used before making any cut. The finishing is more sleek and mature as it is done with matte.

Comparing Various Cricut Machines

Explore 3 and Explore 2 air are the most famous in the mid-range. The Cricut Maker and Cricut Maker 3 are higher-end models for a more extensive range of items and use more techniques than the Explore model. Finally, the Joy is Cricut's lowest version, making it handy, quick to organize, and then use.

Compatibility Blade and Tools for Cricut Explore

Fine Point blade – it is best used only for Cricut Maker 3

Deep Point blade – it is best used only for Cricut Maker 3

Bonded Fabric blade – it is best used only forCricutMaker3

Foil Transfer Kit – it is best used only forCricutMaker3

Rotary blade – it is best for only the Cricut Maker.

Knife blade – This is best for only the Cricut Maker.

Quick Swap Perforation blade – This is best for only the Cricut Maker.

Quick Swap Wavy blade – This best works for the Cricut Maker.

Basic Tools

Here are some Cricut essential tools:

Spatula

It accurately lifts graphics from the Cricut cutting board, avoiding ripping or bending of complex images.

Scraper

It was created specifically to remove undesirable scraps from Cricut cutting mats, resulting in a longer-lasting mat. It could also be used to polish substances like plastic to eliminate tiny bubbles and wrinkling or smoothen things onto the mat.

Scissors

It typically has stainless steel blades formed for longevity and beautiful, uniform cuts.

Tweezers

Their reversed gripping design raises and secures in one phase: compress the handles together to open, then release pressure to clamp together. Polished inside points help keep your fabrics from ripping or being marred.

Changing the Blade

1. Take your Cricut machine's blade housing out.

2. Carefully pull out the blade from the base by gently pushing the pin on the housing.

3. Eliminate the new blade's protective layer.

4. Replace the blade in the housing. The replacement blade will be held in place by the magnet in the housing.

5. Put the blade housing back into the machine.

What are Cricut smart materials?

These smart materials effortlessly go with the machine. They have been created to work without a mat. Cutting is made easier with these Smart materials, and it helps save time and prevent the stress of constantly adjusting the mat.

These Smart materials include the Smart Paper Sticker Card Stock, Smart Iron-On, Smart Vinyl, and Transfer Tape, available for you, along with a free trial to Cricut Access. With Cricut Access, you can access 100 ready-to-do projects to practice with.

Smart Vinyl is available in various lengths, with a maximum length and cutting width of 75 feet and 12 feet, respectively. It may be cut in lengths of up to 12 feet at once, conserving a significant amount of time and material. In addition, your Smart Vinyl has a thick adhesive back that works better than a mat.

Smart Iron-On is available in various sizes with a maximum length and a cutting width of 9 feet and 11.7 feet, respectively. The maximum area for cutting Smart Paper is 11.7 feet long and 11.2 feet wide. Transfer tape helps transfer a ready design from the sheet to the holder material.

It is essential to note that while you have Smart materials to work with the Explore 3, it still accepts regular materials. However, cutting is faster, easier, and more precise with smart materials.

How to set up a Cricut Explore 3 for Mac and Windows

After plugging your machine, it is time to set it up completely. Of course, setting your Explore 3 or any of your Cricut machines entirely depends on the device. Follow the instructions below to get your machine set up on either a Mac, Windows, iOS, or Android. It automatically links your machine to your account when you finish the setup.

Here's a step-by-step guide for setting up and creating amazing crafts.

1. Visit https://design.cricut.com on your browser. Then, download and install Cricut design space for your PC.

2. Next is to sign up or sign in if you have a pre-existing account already.

3. Fill in your accurate details in the spaces provided.

4. You will arrive at a welcome page. Next, click on the hamburger button at the top left to open up a sidebar.

5. Click on 'New Product Setup' to connect to your PC.

6. Select a product type, select 'Smart Cutting Machine.'

7. You will be asked to select which Cricut machine you want to connect. Look out for Cricut Explore 3, select it.

8. (a) It's recommended to keep a distance of 10 inches between the

wall outlet and the Cricut Explorer 3 machine.

Prepare Workspace

Step 1. Clear 10 inches (25 cm) of space behind Cricut Explore™ 3

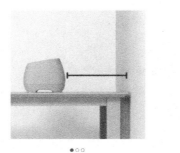

● ○ ○

8. (b) Plug it into the wall outlet and turn it on.

Find an Outlet

Step 2. Plug Cricut Explore™ 3 into wall outlet and power on.

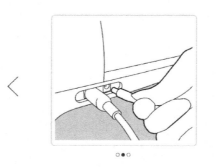

○ ● ○

8. (c) Using the USB
cable, connect the Cricut
Explore 3 machine to your
computer. Click continue
once all connections have
been done.

Connect to Computer

included USB cord to connect Cricut Voldemort™ t

○ ○ ●

9. Next up, register the machine by
confirming your email and
agreeing to the terms of use and

policy of Cricut. Finally, click register to register your machine.

Register Machine

Add Explore 3 to your Cricut ID

paige_joanna_calvert@live.co.uk

Not your email?

10. You will see a successful message showing that your Explore 3 is registered and set up. Click next.

Success!

Your Explore 3 is registered and set up.

11. You can decide to start a 1-month free trial that gives you access to unlimited images, fonts, and designs; or skip it altogether.

12. Here, you can click the green button that says 'New Product' to start designing from scratch or use any ready-made templates.

13. Clicking on 'New Product' brings you to this design space to start designing your crafts.

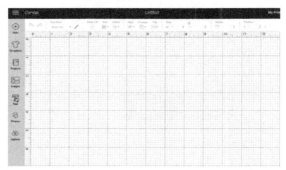

Easy peasy lemon squeezy, right? It's that easy to use. What if you want to pair your device with the Cricut machine via Bluetooth? I got you covered.

- Make sure your Cricut Explore 3 machine is powered on and close to your mobile device or PC.
- Check your mobile device or PC to turn on your Bluetooth as the Cricut Explore 3 always has its Bluetooth enabled.

- Click on add Bluetooth or other devices on your mobile device and PC and wait for your device to detect your Cricut machine. Then, select the machine from the list.
- You may be asked to input a PIN, type 0000. Select connect.
- Your Cricut Explore 3 is now paired with your mobile device or PC.

But, what if there are multiple Cricut machines around with their Bluetooth all enabled? How do you know which to pair and connect with? Not a problem. Look out for the Cricut machine code on the bottom of the machine on the serial number tag. Then, you can match the code to connect to the right Cricut machine Bluetooth's code that's the exact match.

Using Bluetooth

You can connect via Bluetooth by doing this:

- For Windows (mainly Windows 10)
    1. Power on the Explore 3 and ensure it is within 10 feet of your computer.
    2. Ensure your computer is Bluetooth enabled.
    3. To do this, go to Device Manager from the Start Button
    4. Bluetooth is enabled on your PC if it is indicated

there. If not, you will need to buy a Bluetooth Dongle to allow your computer to work with other Bluetooth devices.

5. Once it is listed back, go back to home and open the Settings app.

6. Go to the Devices section.

7. Go to Bluetooth and other devices. Ensure the Bluetooth is on and click on Add Bluetooth or other devices.

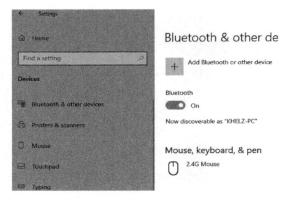

8. Wait for the computer to scan and locate the Explore 3. Then, click on Explore 3 and connect.

9. If asked for a pin to connect, input '0000' as the pin. Then Connect.

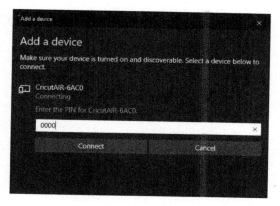

10. You have successfully connected your Cricut Explore 3 to your desktop.

- **For Mac**

    1. Power on the Explore 3 and ensure it is within 10 feet of your computer.

    2. Ensure your computer is Bluetooth enabled. However, most of these computers are Bluetooth enabled.

3. To do this, go to System Preferences from the Apple Menu and search for the Bluetooth option.

4. Click on the Bluetooth option and ensure it's on.

5. It would scan for other Bluetooth options.

6. Pair with the Explore 3 and use the pin '0000' to connect.

- **For iOS**

  1. Power on the Explore 3 and ensure it is within 10 feet of your computer.

  2. Go to Settings and click on the Bluetooth option.

3. Ensure the Bluetooth is on and look for the Cricut machine.

4. Use the pin '0000' to pair.

5. Your pairing is successful.

- **For Android**

   1. Power on the Explore 3 and ensure it is within 10 feet of your computer.

   2. Go to Settings and click on the Bluetooth option.

   3. Ensure the Bluetooth is on and look for the Cricut machine.

   4. Use the pin '0000' to pair.

   5. Your pairing is successful.

Pairing and Unpairing the machine with a computer

Whenever you wish to pair the Explore 3 with your computer, you can use either the USB cable or via Bluetooth. For a Mac, you might need a USB converter.

To unpair, follow the instructions below depending on your device.

- **For Windows**

  1. Open the Settings app from the Home menu.
  2. Go to the Devices section.
  3. Go to the Bluetooth and other devices option.
  4. Select the device to remove and click Remove
  5. You have successfully unpaired your machine from your computer.

- **For Mac**

  1. From the Apple menu, go to System Preferences.

  2. Click the Bluetooth option.

  3. Choose the device to remove and click the Remove icon (x).

  4. You have successfully unpaired your machine from your computer.

- **For iOS**

  1. Navigate to Bluetooth from Settings.

  2. Click the info icon next to the device you want to remove/forget.

  3. You'll be given the option to Forget This Device based on the device's current status.

- **For Android**
    1. Navigate to Bluetooth from Settings.
    2. If your Bluetooth is turned off, put it on.
    3. To the right of your Cricut machine in the list, click on the Settings icon.
    4. Click the Forget button.

You would have to follow the pairing instruction again to pair back.

Resetting

You can reset your machine by doing so on Cricut Design Space. First, highlight all the files from the Local Data folder, then press Shift+Delete to delete them permanently.

On the upper-left corner of the menu, click on View, then Force Reload. This permanently resets everything in your Design Space App. Do not attempt to reset if you do not wish to lose your designs and settings.

Obtaining the most recent version

It is recommended to always use the most recent version of Cricut Design Space for the best possible results. To find the current version, follow the following steps;

- **For Windows**
    1. Look at the bottom right of the taskbar and tap the hidden app's icon (an upward arrow icon).
    2. Hover on the Design Space app.
    3. The current version of the app will show.

- **For Mac**
    1. In the top left corner of the screen, click the Cricut icon.
    2. Choose "About."
    3. A tiny pop-up displaying the current version will appear.

- **For iOS**

  1. Sign in to the Cricut Design Space app.

  2. Open the application menu at the top left corner of the screen.

  3. At the bottom of the menu, you will see the current version number.

- **For Android**

  1. Sign in to the Cricut Design Space app.

  2. Click on the menu bar (person icon) at the upper left corner of the screen.

  3. At the bottom of the menu, you will see the current version number.

Finding the current framework of the machine

1. Power on your machine and sign into Cricut Design Space.
2. From the menu at the top-left corner, choose Update the Firmware.
3. A list of machines shows from which you choose your machine. Unfortunately, it takes some time before it can recognize your machine.
4. A pop-up will alert you when your machine has been recognized that your firmware is up to date. If it is not, it will request an update.

Choosing material settings

When your Cricut Explore 3 machine is connected to your computer or mobile device, the material settings are shown as a sequence of rectangular boxes. Select the box to change the settings if you see your material.

- **For Mac/Windows**

From Browse all materials, you can search by Category or Property. At the bottom of the page, you will find the Material Settings, where you can edit the material's Cut Pressure, Multi-cut, or Blade Type.

- **For iOS/Android**

From All materials, you can search by Category or Property. At the bottom of the page, you will find the Material

Settings, where you can edit the material's Cut Pressure, Multi-cut, or Blade Type.

Custom cut settings

The Cricut Explore 3 machine is compatible with 100 different materials. Therefore, the design space already has a pre-computerized set of instructions for each material.

If you want to create custom cut settings, follow the following steps:

1. Sign in and create a new project.
2. Ensure your machine is powered on and connected to your account.

3. Go to the Make it option to preview your design when you are done, and press Continue.

4. The next step is the Set Material where it prompts you to choose a material out of the given ones. Then, on your Mac/Windows, you go to the Browse All Materials section to search for your material. With iOS/Android, it is the All Materials button.

5. If you do not see your material from the app menu, navigate to Manage Custom materials, and towards the bottom of the page, select Material Settings.

6. Select Add New Materials from the bottom of the page. Give it a name and save it.

7. You can edit the settings of any material of your choice. From the

Material Settings page, you see an Edit option on the list of each material. Click on it.

8. You can edit the Cut Pressure, Multi-cut, or Blade Type of the material.

9. Save the edit and close (x) the page.

10. You have successfully created your custom setting for your materials, and you can begin your cut.

Matless cutting ability

While in previous models, except the Cricut Joy, you have to load your material using a mat, in the Cricut Explore 3 and Maker 3, there is no need for that.

Some improvisions were made to cut Vinyl without a mat in these previous models; however, Design Space restrained the material size to 12 by 24 feet. But with Explore 3, those restrictions do not hold.

You can create large sizes of the design, as long as 75 feet, and the fantastic thing about it is that all you need to do is load the material, and it begins to cut out your design. So the inconvenience of always joining your materials together while trying to adjust it on the mat is gone. Now is a new era for matless unlimited cutting!

Cleaning your Cricut Explore 3

It is usual for the machine to accumulate grease and dust over time as it is being used. To clean your Explore 3;

1. Make sure it isn't plugged into a power source.

2. With a clean piece of material, spray a decent portion of a plastic sprayer on the cloth and use it to clean the machine's body.

3. Debris may accumulate on or in your machine but ensure you wipe these particles away with a clean cloth.

4. Carefully remove it using a cotton swab, tissue, or soft cloth.

CHAPTER THREE

Setting up Design Space

With the fantastic features available for designers in the Cricut design space, some users find installing or downloading the app/software difficult. If you are in this category, fret not.

An easy-to-follow guide has been put together below to guide you on how you can install the Cricut design space on your computer. The app can be used on a PC and various tablets and smartphones, including iPhone and Android devices.

You can install the app using the steps below:

Step 1: An internet connection is required to download or install this application successfully, so you need to have one.

Step 2: For Android or iOS devices, go over to Google Playstore or AppStore and search for "Cricut Design Space." You will find the app among the search results, and then you can proceed to download and install the Cricut design space on your device.

You can install the design space software to your desktop browser: Visit design.cricut.com and select download; your download should start almost immediately. You can monitor your download progress under the "Downloads" tab.

Once completed, double-click on the downloaded file and install it. On Mac PCs, begin the installation by double-clicking on the .dmg file in the "Downloads" tab and dragging the Cricut icon to the Applications folder icon.

You should see an installation progress bar on your screen as the installation goes on. Windows may ask for permission and trust for the installation process, select "Yes" or "Trust this application," and proceed.

Step 3: When the installation is completed, you can launch the Cricut design space app/software and sign in or sign-up.

For iOS devices, options for "New Machine Setup" and "App Overview" will display on the launch screen. Skip this if you want to sign in or sign up and start designing.

If app download fails to begin on Android devices using Google PlayStore, you might want to free up some space on your device so you can proceed with the download.

How to Make Use of Design Space

Since we have gone through the basics of installing Cricut Design Space, we might also explore the various available features using design space. Cricut Design Space can be described as the wholesome app/software for designers and creatives. It has endless possibilities that can be achieved when designing, mainly when used alongside the Cricut Machine.

Below are several functions that could be utilized with the Design Space and how to use them:

Welding Tool: How to Weld

The welding tool on the Cricut design space is used to join two or more characters to form a single piece that can easily be movable. Characters that could be joined can be letters, numbers, shapes, pictures, etc. To use this tool;

1.) Firstly, add the characters you want to weld together to your design panel. Then, arrange the characters on the panel the exact way you would want them to look when they're welded together. You can weld as many characters together as you like.

2.) Click and drag your cursor to completely highlight the entire area where your characters are. Ensure that every part of the characters you want to be highlighted is completely covered.

3.) Finally, click on the Weld tool option on the design space interface to weld your selected characters together. It is located in the lower right-hand corner of the screen.

Slicing Tool: How to Slice

The slicing tool is another exciting tool in the design space used to cut shapes, letters, pictures, or any desired character(s) into preferred shapes or patterns. The tool slices into pretty much anything. To use this tool,

1.) Add your preferred shape, text, picture, or character you would want to cut to your design panel.

To explain this procedure, this example shows how to cut/slice out a heart shape from the middle of a square. Then, you can add the heart shape and position it where you want the heart shape cut out on the square.

2.) Next, click and drag your cursor over the area of both shapes on the design panel to highlight them.

3.) Proceed to select the slice tool at the right bottom corner of your design space interface. It is possible to only slice through a single layer or character.

Once you have clicked on the slice tool, the slicing process has been completed. You can now remove your initial heart shape from inside the square, and the original part of the square is cut in a heart shape to reveal your heart-shaped slice.

Flattening Tool: How to Flatten

The flattening tool reduces a cut file to a print and cut image. This means that it turns multiple layers of an image into a single layer. It's that simple. To use this feature;

1.) Attach the cut file to your design canvas. For example purposes, you can add a basic shape like a square to your design canvas and insert any image from the Cricut design space.

Now on your design panel, you have a cut file.

2.) Highlight the entire area of these on the design canvas. This selects the image you want to flatten.

3.) Click on the flatten tool. It is located at the bottom right corner of your Cricut design interface.

Boom! You have just flattened your desired image.

How to Attach Using Cricut Design Space

The Attach feature of the Cricut Design Space can be used in several cases. It is used to maintain a design format to become uniform and appear on the Cricut machine the same way it appears on the design canvas. To use this feature,

1.) Add your desired set of words, stickers, emojis, characters, etc., onto your design panel.

2.) Arrange them in your desired format.

3.) Select and pull your cursor over the area of both shapes on the design panel to highlight them.

4.) Proceed to click on the Attach tool. This way, when you proceed to make it, everything appears on the Cricut machine the same way it appears on your design canvas.

How to Upload Images to Design Space

It is pretty easy to upload images to the Cricut design space. To do this,

1.) Click on Upload on the left panel of your Cricut design space interface. Using this method, you can upload images of different formats —JPG, JIF, PNG, SVG, BMP, and DXF.

2.) Proceed to click on the "Upload Image" option and choose your desired image which you would like to add from your device's library, or you can click, drag, and drop your desired image into the design canvas.

4.) When this is done, you will be presented with a list of formats in which your image will appear on the canvas —

Simple, Moderately Complex, and Complex. Of course, whichever one you pick, you can always undo your selection by clicking on the "Back" button at the bottom left of your screen.

5.) You can also select and erase portions of your image that you want to remove. Finally, you will be prompted to choose how to save your uploaded image —either as a print and cut image or as a cut image. Saving it as a cut image saves your image and each design on your image as a special character on it and vice versa.

6.) Once this is completed, you can click on "Insert Images," and you will find your newly uploaded image ready to be inserted into your design canvas. This saves you the stress of having to upload the image again.

How to Import SVG Files into Cricut Design Space

Uploading SVG images employs a different method from uploading regular image formats like JPG or PNG. However, this does not mean that uploading SVG images are impossible. On the contrary, they are even easier to upload. You can upload SVG images with the following steps.

1.) Firstly, click on Upload on the left panel of your Cricut design space interface.

2.) Add your desired SVG image from your device's library.

3.) Because SVG files come in two different pieces, the entire process of selecting and erasing parts of the uploaded image is skipped, so it's pretty easy from here. Just proceed to add your selected image.

4.) Once this is completed, you can click on "Insert Images," and you will find your newly uploaded image ready to be inserted into your design canvas.

How to Edit Images in Cricut Design Space

This is not a usual one-size-fits-all procedure. Editing a picture usually requires a designer's creativity and largely depends on what they want to achieve. Cricut design space allows designers and creatives to express their ingenuity by providing various tools and functions at their disposal.

After uploading their desired image for editing, Editors can proceed to "Advanced Options" to explore a variety of changes that could spice up their image.

How to Group and Ungroup

The group and ungroup features work similarly to the Attach tool with a few variations. The group function allows users to select two or more images, text, pictures, characters, etc., as one to allow for uniform changes and modifications across all grouped characters.

However, unlike the attach function, this grouping function does not reflect on the cutting machine. Grouped characters or images will appear ungrouped on the cutting machine. To use this feature;

1.) Add your desired set of words, stickers, emojis, characters, etc., onto your design panel.

2.) Arrange them in your desired format.

3.) Select and pull your cursor over the area of both shapes on the design panel to highlight them.

4.) Proceed to click on the group tool. You can follow this same procedure to ungroup your grouped characters or images.

How to make a stencil

Even for beginner designers, making a stencil on the Cricut design space should be pretty easy. A stencil is a thin material with a design cut out of it, typically plastic, vinyl, or paper. Paint over the sheet to use a stencil. Only the cut-out parts of the stencil will allow the paint to pass through, transferring the design to the surface.

Making stencils with the Cricut machine is pretty easy. First, you need to design your stencil on the Cricut design canvas. When this is done, you can then cut out unwanted parts from the stencil, apply it on your preferred surface and then paint on it.

Getting Started With Text

With Cricut Design Space, designers and creatives can do more with a wide variety of text functions. From a list of over 400 fonts available for use, designers can now create and personalize their projects.

To start using the text tool, add your project. This will open up a text box to type your words or letters into. Doing this will also present options for you to format your text with such as fonts, font size, color, etc. You can also add your desired fonts or write a text yourself using the Cricut pen. With Cricut design space, you are in total control of your design.

Editing text menu tool

After the text has been added to your Cricut design panel, an array of options automatically displays that allows you to twitch, modify, adjust and change the text format to suit your desired editing needs. The options included in the text editing menu tool include

Font: This is used to change the text font from the default font Cricut design space uses. A lot of font options are available for use. Some fonts, however, can only be accessed with a Cricut Access subscription.

Letter Spacing Option: this allows you to change the distance between each letter. You can also type in the number or use the up and down arrows, and Cricut design space will change the space between each letter for you to view.

Alignment Tool: This helps align text to either left, center, or right of your text box.

There are also advanced editing text options that lets you group, ungroup and curve text.

Offset text tool

This feature allows users to offset text to beautify it. This feature adds an extra layer of the text or character as an outline to the background of the text and allows users to increase or reduce the offset size. To use this function,

1.) Click and drag your cursor over the area of both shapes on the design panel to highlight them.

2.) Proceed to select the offset option and a set of options to increase or decrease offset size and a variety of other options.

Curve text tool and how to curve text

1.) You can use fonts and other assets from Envato elements with an extensive collection of professional quality fonts and images. You can download and get to work with it right away. First, however, make sure that you install the fonts you want to use.

2.) Open up Cricut design space, and you'll be presented with a home screen window. Click new project to create the canvas for the project

3.) Next step is to add some text to the design canvas. Click the text icon, and you will be presented with a text box with which you can then type down any text you want to.

4.) When text has been added successfully, you can choose to change the font of the text. Make sure your text is selected, and click on the font drop-down on the top left corner to choose a new font.

5.) Proceed to click the handle till you're satisfied, then release the click of the mouse button.

Now that your text is curved, you will likely want to adjust it in various ways. You'll get mixed results on this depending on the font you have used and its natural letter spacing. You can change the letter spacing by adequately using the arrows by the letter spacing. You may also want to rotate too. You can do this by clicking on the rotate icon when the text is selected.

Text alignment tool

Text alignment tool is used to justify text characters or letters to fit the designer's standard. To use this feature,

1.) Add your desired set of words, stickers, emojis, characters, etc., onto your design panel.

2.) Highlight the piece of the text you want to align by clicking and dragging your cursor over the text area.

3.) Proceed to click on the align tool at the top of your Cricut Design Panel, and you will be presented with a list of alignment options and formats.

4.) Select your desired alignment format, and your text should be aligned successfully. It's that easy!

Font size and letter spacing

This feature is used to change text writing glyphs. Each font has a unique design created to suit various user specifications. They also have different sizes depending on designer preferences.

You can toggle your preferred font sizes to suit your design needs as a designer.

Click on the font size menu to add text to choose. Font sizes are represented in numbers. You can also type in your preferred font size value if it isn't included in the drop-down menu.

Advanced options

How to Add a Font

This feature is for users with specific fonts they would like to use on a project, not among the Cricut Design fonts available. To upload a font,

1.) Visit your preferred online font store or website and download your desired font to your computer/PC. This allows you have your desired font offline on your PC.

2.) Once downloaded, open it either as an OTF font or as a TTFN font. For Mac users, you can select the option of using an OTF, while PC users can choose to use either one. Double-click on the font and select install font. This should add the font to your font book on your computer.

3.) Go over to Cricut Design Space and click "Text," then search for the name of the just downloaded font in the search bar. If it doesn't appear among the search results, don't fret. Instead, sign out of Cricut Design Space and sign back in with new project. After this, your newly added font should appear in your Cricut Design Space when you search for it.

How to use a contour tool

The contour tool hides different layers of an image yet still retains the remaining parts of the image. This can be used when a designer wants just a specific part of a picture but doesn't want the rest and vice versa. To use this function;

1.) Attach the desired image to the design canvas.

2.) Highlight the added image by clicking and dragging the mouse over the image area on the design canvas.

3.) Once the image is highlighted, click on the contour at the right bottom corner of the design interface.

4.) This should present you with an interface where you can click on unwanted parts of the image to hide contour.

5.) When completed, exit the hide contour interface, and you should see what's left of your desired image on your design panel.

How to assess and add special characters in design space

Special characters are used to add designs and style to text format. Users can use special characters to write text using an additional set of crafted letters and characters as an alternative to font selection. To access special characters in the Cricut design space,

1.) Add your desired font to your design space. For Mac users, this can be done with a program called Fontslab. Windows users can use Character Maps UWP.

2.) Open Characters Map and search for the same font you added on your design space, copy the specific letter with the special character you want to add, and replace them one by one onto your design space.

3.) When completely done, you can click on group to arrange all the characters.

How to uninstall Cricut Design Space

Cricut Design Space can be uninstalled in four basic steps.

1.) Completely close the Design Space application on your Desktop

2.) Search for "Programs" under the Start menu of your desktop and click on it.

3.) Under "Programs," select "Add or remove programs." The Apps & Features" window will open.

4.) Search for the Cricut Design Space, select the app and click "Uninstall."

5.) Confirm your desire to uninstall the application and proceed.

Mac users can easily select the Cricut app under Applications and drag it to the trash to uninstall. However, users might want to click Empty Trash to delete the application permanently.

CHAPTER FOUR

TYPES OF VINYL

When it comes to crafting with vinyl, many types of vinyl can be used with your cutting machine, and many times it can be confusing which you should use for a particular project. Though, the type of vinyl to be used depends on personal preference and aesthetics. Let's go deeper into the types of vinyl and which would be suitable for a particular project.

There are two types of vinyl; adhesive vinyl and heat transfer vinyl, popularly known as HTV.

Adhesive Vinyl

Adhesive vinyl is a sticky vinyl that adheres to surfaces without applying heat. It is perfect for cups, decals, signs, tumblers, and cars. Adhesive vinyl comes in colors, sizes, thickness, and brands. Based on adhesiveness, there are two sub-categories;

- Permanent Adhesive Vinyl: can withstand stress and stick to surfaces permanently.
- Removable Adhesive Vinyl: has a limit to which it handles stress and can be removed easily.

There are many types of adhesive vinyl based on brands, but the most used brand is Oracal. Oracal 631 and 651 is the brand most crafters start with.

Oracal 631 is used for indoor purposes like walls, picture frames boxes, and anything that won't be washed to avoid coming off easily. It lasts for 2 years and can be removed without stress when you don't need it anymore.

Oracal 651 is used for outdoor purposes like your cars. It lasts for 8 years, making it the ideal choice for your car decals or items you would like to wash— things such as your cups, mugs, etc.

Adhesive vinyl is put through a die cutter on top of the paper carrier with the vinyl. Once your design has been cut out, the extra vinyl left is pulled away through a process called 'weeding.' Next, transfer tape is applied to the design, the paper under it is removed as the decal is applied. Once applied, the transfer tape is pulled off.

Heat Transfer Vinyl

Also called HTV or Iron-on Vinyl, it adheres to surfaces with heat application. It's not sticky like the adhesive vinyl and a perfect choice for fabrics like coats, blankets, shirts, bags, stuffed animals, etc. This is why heat must be applied if the vinyl material stays without coming off. An iron can heat press these materials, hence 'Iron-on Vinyl.' Like adhesive vinyl, there are varieties of HTV available, but crafters most use Cricut among the brands.

Cricut HTV offers 5 types based on texture though there are others.

- Foil: It has a surface that shines.
- Holographic: It has a surface with color-changing effects.
- Everyday: It has a plain surface perfect for beginners.

- Patterned: It has prints and patterns on its surface.
- Mesh: It is a durable vinyl commonly used on jerseys.

How To Weed Cricut Iron-on Vinyl

Weeding is the next step after the HTV has been cut by the Cricut machine and the last step before your project is transferred to the item. Weeding means getting rid of the excess parts not needed on the design. Cricut has a curved hook tool for this. Using your hands will mess the project up; with the curved hook, you can pull out the unwanted part without it going down. I would recommend you get a 'Cricut weeding set'; it comes with many tools to make you weed out your project with ease. Check out these easy steps on how to weed Cricut Iron-on Vinyl;

1. First, get the corner of your design with your curved hook tool and pull it out.

2. Pull it out from a 45-degree angle.

3. You should be able to see your design now

4. Hold your project to the light to see the lines in the design to weed out. You can also look at your design on the design space to see the image to know where exactly you should weed out.

5. Once you know the points on your project to weed out, slowly take the pieces out using the curved hook.

6. You should have all pieces out and ready to apply your design to the item.

How To Apply Cricut Iron-On Vinyl

1. You need a heat guide before you apply your Cricut Iron-on. Head to www.cricut.com/en_us/heatguide, and it will bring you right here; click on the right easy press you are using.

Heat Guide

Select options to view instructions.

Cricut
EasyPress Mini

Cricut
EasyPress 2

Cricut
EasyPress

Which Cricut EasyPress do I have? Find out here.

Heat-Transfer Material

Select heat-transfer material ⌄

2. Scroll down to select the heat transfer material. In this case, it will be the Everyday iron-on

3. Next is to pick the base material from the list of materials here. I'm using 100% cotton, which I'm picking.

4. Now, you are to choose what is underneath your base material. Depending on which you are

using, you can pick between the Cricut EasyPress Mat or a Towel. Click apply.

5. Here, you will be told what to do to transfer your design to your material. First, you need to preheat the base material for 5s to eliminate any moisture that may exist.

6. Then put back your design on the base material and heat at 315°F for the 30s using light pressure.

7. Once the 30s are up, flip the cotton to the other side and heat-press for 15s.

8. Now, you 'Warm peel.' This means you don't have to peel it out when it's very hot so that you don't burn your

hands and you don't need to wait till it's cold. Instead, you have to peel it off while it is still warm. Do this slowly.

9. There you go. You've got your design on your item. Cheers!

How to Use a Cricut to Cut Vinyl

Once you are done designing, the next step is to cut your material.

1. Get your Cricut mat. Remove the protective cover.

2. Line the material along the gridline of your mat.

3. Put it into the machine and make sure it is gripped properly.

4. Click on the double arrows button to firmly hold the material during cutting and easily remove the material from the mat.

5. Turn the mat over to a flat surface after your Cricut Explore 3 has finished cutting.

6. Slowly pull the mat straight up until the material is removed.

There you go, easy peasy lemon squeezy. Now you have your design all cut out for you.

CHAPTER FIVE

Cricut Explore Projects

Unlike regular bags, tote bags can be used on different occasions like shopping, work or school beach bags, or picnics can be carried along to the gym center, as traveling bags, laundry bags, and much more. In addition, tote bags are unique and portable; they come in different sizes, colors, and designs.

How to Use Cricut Infusible Ink to Create Designs on Tote Bags

STEP 1- Create a Design

⇒ The first step is to create a design of your choice with a phone or laptop using software applications meant for designs like the Cricut joy app, Corel draw, Canva, Adobe Photoshop, etc.

⇒ If your Design consists of numbers or words, make sure to increase the font size to be visible on the tote bag.

⇒ Keep making iterations on your Design until you achieve designs suitable to your taste.

STEP 2

⇒ Place the liner side of the infusible ink transfer sheet in a standard grip mat.

⇒ Ensure that size of the design fit on tote bags blank.

⇒ If using a Cricut Explore machine, pick an infusible ink transfer sheet and turn the smart set dial to custom.

STEP 3

⇒ Place the mat and blade in the machine and switch on the machine.

STEP 4

⇒ Remove the design from mat and trim the sheets unused area.

STEP 5

⇒ Lint-roll the entire surface area to eliminate any moisture or grease that could damage the work

⇒ Place the cardstock inside and outside the tote bag; this is done to protect the product from being burnt.

⇒ Apply heat on the surface using the EasyPress for 15 seconds; the temperature should be about 195°C.

⇒ After heating, allow designs to dry completely.

STEP 6

⇒ Apply the butcher paper (paper with the Design printed on it).

⇒ Heat the surface area at the temperature range of 195°C for about 40 seconds using light pressure.

⇒ Slowly raise the pressure applied by the Cricut and allow it to cool completely.

⇒ Then remove the butcher paper when cool and your beautiful tote bag is ready.

Book Covering With Cricut Foil Transfer Kit

It is often said, "*Do not judge a book by its cover,*" but let's face it, one of the determining factors before reading a book is its covering. A lovely book covering can captivate a reader to purchase the book and read it. Are you planning to release a book soon? The next section is just for you; you'll see how to create a beautiful book covering with a **Cricut foil transfer kit.**

STEP 1

⇒ Take measurements of the book you will be covering (length, breadth, and surface area).

⇒ Create the Design you want, including the title, the author's last name (not compulsory).

⇒ Adjust the font size to fit in with the book in question.

⇒ Choose Foil from the Operation drop-down menu in the top toolbar after selecting the text created from the box (under the Draw section). Then choose Medium (If you're designing with Canva).

STEP 2

⇒ Place a sheet of 12 by 24 textured card stock on a Light Grip mat

⇒ Place a foil transfer sheet in the middle

⇒ Pull the foil tightly so it's nice and taut.

STEP 3

⇒ Adjusting text In Design Space by changing the mat size to 12 by 24

⇒ Ensure that it is firm.

STEP 3

⇒ Ensure that the Cricut Foil Transfer Tool presses down on the foil sheet to imprint it on the paper. Then, after the transfer process, you peel the foil off, and the words are magically on your cardstock.

STEP 4 -Turning Cardstock to a Book Cover

⇒ Stand the book up on its spine over the foil title. Mark the end of the book.

⇒ Align the book's spine onto the trimmed cardstock again, and double-check your title's position.

⇒ Make a fold line on the cardstock on two corners of the book spine a few times. Follow the lines to fold the paper inward, then outward, to get a nice clean fold line.

STEP 5

⇒ Put the book in the spine folds, then use the scoring stylus again to create your fold lines for the front and back of the book. Next, fold the paper into the front and back covers of the book. Trim if necessary.

⇒ Finally, use the scoring stylus gently to score the indent beside the spine on the front and back.

⇒ Carefully and loosely pressed the indent once with the scoring stylus tip angled, lay the stylus on its side, and slid it back and forth.

Making A T-Shirt With Iron-On Vinyl

Before moving on to how you can make a T-shirt with Iron-on **Vinyl**, let us first discuss what the word Iron-on **Vinyl** means. **Iron-on vinyl** is a fabric-adhesive vinyl that requires heat to activate the glue on vinyl. Vinyl comes in different forms like sheets, rolls, and bundles.

Necessary Items

- Scissors

- Cutting machine

- Iron

- Cutting mat

- Iron board

- T-shirt

- A Thin towel or light plank

- Tweezers.

STEP 1

⇒ In every design making, the first step is to create the design of your choice, using software applications meant for designs. Like Canva, Adobe Photoshop, to mention a few.

⇒ Mirror the design by clicking on the rotation icon of your design software.

⇒ Delete the original design and drag the other design you mirrored to the screen for a proper view.

⇒ Resize the design to fit your need.

STEP 2

⇒ Cut the vinyl according to the design required for the T-shirt. Note that when cutting the vinyl for your fabric, consider the machine size for the design you want to create.

⇒ Place the shiny side of the vinyl on the mat and place it on the cutting machine to load the design on the vinyl's surface—press load on the cutting machine's body.

⇒ After the Design is achieved, press the unload button to remove the Design from the cutting machine.

STEP 3

⇒ Use scissors and tweezers to trim the unwanted part and remove the Design.

STEP 4

⇒ Preheat the surface of the fabrics to make them smooth.

⇒ Place the trimmed Design on the cloth together with a hard surface or a piece of towel, but hard surfaces like wood-like light plans are mostly preferred.

⇒ Place the iron on the surface and heat for 5 seconds, applying pressure on the iron.

⇒ Allow for 10 seconds to cool

STEP 5

- Gently peel off the carrier sheet, and your T-shirt is ready to be worn. Note: if the heat was correctly applied, the carrier sheet would pull off easily.

Faux Leather Hair Brows

Faux leather hair brows are artificial eyebrows made from leathers and sometimes hairs extracted from animals and other materials. It is mostly used for make-ups, cosmetic purposes, and fashion.

Faux leather hair brows are unisex, meaning both men and women wear them regardless of age. It can add tremendous beauty to the individual using it. During movie sets, this can be applied to the actor or actress depending on the role and requirements of the movie. Others decide to wear them permanently by performing cosmetic surgery in other to fix them.

If you have scanty brows and this is of interest to you, you can book an appointment with a qualified make-up expert to design one just for you, and then you experience how this particular feature adds more glow and beauty to the user.

Engraving Acrylic

Acrylic Engraving is using acrylic glass to create designs on them; it is printing texts or photos on acrylic sheets using an engraving machine.

Source: <u>Weetext</u>

Nature Of Acrylic Glass

Acrylic glass is transparent and looks exactly like glass, but the difference is that acrylic glass is more transparent than regular glasses, making it perfect for engraving work, and errors are easily detected and seen in between the glasses.

Acrylic glass is lighter than normal glass; this makes them portable and easy to carry. They are also described as thermoplastics because they undergo heat when in a molten or near molten form. They are malleable and can be molded to any desired shape; it is also known as **plexiglass**

Uses Of Acrylic Glass

They are used as a gift or trophies in companies; they are used to manufacture nails, lenses, jewelry, bags, shoes, etc. Some hotels use acrylic glass for their food menus; they manufacture logos, business cards, key holders, and furniture. In the medical field, it is used for manufacturing medical devices. So how can you get started in creating your designs on acrylic glass? First, let's talk about things you'll need to get started.

Items Needed

- Tape

- Paper

- Scissors

- A computer and a printer

- Dremel

STEPS TO CREATE YOUR DESIGNS

Step 1. Create your desired Design on the computer using any design software.

Step 2. Flip the Design horizontally to have that mirror view.

Step 3. Print your design on paper using the printer.

Step 4. Trim the unwanted area from work.

Step 5. Place the Design on the acrylic glass surface and tape it.

Step 6. Using the Dremel inscribe the Design to be attached to the acrylic glass.

Step 7. Ensure that the plastic foil is removed before engraving the Design on the acrylic glass.

Note: This method is a simple way of engraving designs on an acrylic glass of which is recommended to try them first as a drag before applying it to your main work.

Custom Coffee Mug

Custom mug coffee can be so mesmerizing, especially when it is personalized. So how can you make your mugs look attractive and full of memories? Let's find out!!

STEP 1 - CHOOSING A MUG

⇒ When choosing a mug for your designs, ensure there are no writings on your mugs in other to make the Design pronounced.

⇒ wash and dry them before designing them

STEP 2 - CREATE A DESIGN

⇒ You can either create them or search online for a design you like, copy and edit them to a desirable size.

⇒ Print the Design.

⇒ Cut and trim them to the desired size to fit the mug.

STEP 3 - PAINT THE BACKGROUND

⇒ If you aren't cool with the color of the mug, you can change the color of the mug with **Acrylic paint**. When choosing the color for the paint, it should not conflict with the colors used for the Design you wish to apply.

⇒ After painting, allow it to dry

STEP 4 - TRANSFER DESIGN TO THE MUG

⇒ Place the paper on the mug

⇒ Using pencil wax, follow the design lines and draw them accordingly. Ensure that all the designs are inscribed on the mug.

⇒ Allow designs to dry.

⇒ If you wish to inscribe some writings, you can use the pencil wax to create some writings on the mug

⇒ You can also apply stickers as designs for the mugs.

Frequently Asked Questions

1. Why are the tote bags named "tote" bags?

They are named tote bags because they are potent and sturdy and can carry heavy loads. Strong materials were used to create them because of their purpose (carrying heavy items).

2. Tote bags and handbags which are the best?

All bags are unique and have different purposes; it is best recommended to go for your preference and according to what you want to use them.

3. Is there any other alternative apart from the cutting machine?

Cutting machine gives you clean and neat work, but an alternative is using scissors, razor blades, or knives.

4. What material is best used for a T-shirt?

T-shirts can be made with different fabrics, but cotton fabrics are mostly preferred because of their long-lasting nature.

CONCLUSION

So for beginner designers, the Cricut Design space is simply a complimentary design software application used to create, edit and design projects using the Cricut machine.

Cricut design machine makes it possible for designers of various professional levels —from beginner to expert, to express their outstanding creativity through their designs. Cricut design space lets users layout project designs using pre-designed graphics and fonts with various exciting features. There are also already-made projects on the design space which designers can create and edit.

Cricut design space makes it possible to create unique designs by combining simple shapes. A vast array of fonts are also available for designers in the Cricut design space, creating text-only layouts. Users can also develop and design project ideas and save them on the Cricut design space Access account. It is also possible to customize and develop projects created by other community members using Cricut design space.

As icing on the entire cake of Cricut design space, there are a lot of features and easy to create projects that help amateur designers who want to use Cricut Design Space. Interesting, isn't it?

Are you ready to start your own designs?

Printed in Great Britain
by Amazon